Greek Mythology

The greatest Greek Mythology tales, including gods, goddesses, monsters, heroes, and much more!

Table of Contents

Introduction

Mythology, or the religions of ancient cultures, continue to inspire us today. They were created at a time when people didn't understand the world around them, and so sought to explain it through stories and fantastical interpretations.

While there are arguments among scholars as to how much of these stories were actually believed, how much were allegorical, and how much were simply a form of popular literature at the time, no one can deny the staying power of these stories. Whether it's Celtic, Native American, or Egyptian, the stories and the powerful gods and heroes who populated them continue to inspire and captivate people today.

However, the culture responsible for arguably the most well-known and enduring mythology is Ancient Greece.

From television shows to popular young adult novels, the stories of Greek mythology are some of the most widely known and used. Greek mythology is almost instantly recognizable, and chances are that even if you've never studied mythology or really know much about it, you at least know the basics of who the gods are and some of the myths about them.

What we consider Greek mythology is comprised of the stories of the Greek pantheon and the heroes that interacted with them, developed, and told from around 900-800 BC to about 600 AD. We know as much as we do about Greek mythology and history because the Greeks would often depict their mythologies and historical events on pottery, in temples, and through other visual means, as well as writing them down.

One of the interesting parts of Greek mythology is that it blends with actual Greek history. For example, one of the most famous stories in Greek mythology is the Iliad, an epic poem which depicts a ten-year war between the Greeks and the Trojans. Archeologists have since found where the city of Troy was located and that it was in fact destroyed several times, including around the time that the Iliad describes. But the historical events of the epic are also marked by mythological events, such as the gods helping out various sides, heroes who are immortal, and so on.

So, what is it about Greek mythology that makes it so popular and enduring? A great deal of it is probably because Greek civilization had a huge impact on Western history. The Greeks made huge leaps forward in math and science, and we have information about much of their recorded history, while the recorded history of other ancient civilizations has been lost.

As we move forward in history, we see that the civilizations that came after the Greeks constantly talked about them. Roman mythology, for example, is almost exactly the same as Greek mythology. They even took the twelve gods of Olympus, changed their names, added a few characteristics, and called it a day. During the Renaissance period, there was a huge interest in antiquity, and so many artists were commissioned to do work in the style of Ancient Greek artists and to depict scenes from Greek mythology.

But that doesn't quite explain why those civilizations chose to emulate the Greeks and continue to use their mythology. What is it about the Greek tales of feuding gods, fighting heroes, and terrible trials that so captivated them, and why do they continue to captivate us?

Perhaps it is the idea that these gods were not all-powerful beings, nor were they perfect. Most of the world's modern religions discuss an omnipotent, all-knowing, perfect, singular God. How that God is depicted precisely can vary, depending on whether you're looking at Christianity, Judaism, Islam, Hinduism, or something that doesn't even have a singular God per se, such as Buddhism or Taoism.

But the Greeks told stories about multiple gods that had weaknesses, flaws, and made mistakes just like humans. They had their loves and their losses and their petty fights and their great deeds, just like humans. The Greeks didn't hold gods up as a perfect ideal, but rather as creatures that might have more power than we did, but weren't all that different from us. That humanity and the relationships between the gods, and between gods and mortals, is what is so compelling about Greek mythology and what keeps us reading about it to this day.

And of course, there's that little part of us that likes believing in the idea of fantastical monsters and powerful gods. Humans have always liked to spin their stories, and the fantasy that the Greeks created is fun to indulge in and speculate about— because even though it's not real, we can't help but wonder to ourselves, what if?

And so here are the gods, the heroes, the monsters, and the stories that have captured western civilization for so many years.

Chapter 1: The Myths Of Creation

Every mythology tends to start with a creation myth. In Egypt, this myth is that there was once nothing but a black chaotic sea, until a lotus flower rose up out of the water and bloomed. Inside the lotus flower was the sun god, Ra, who became the first god and led all the others, bringing light to the world.

Many other creation myths tend to say something similar. However, Greek mythology differs in that the first gods created were not the gods that ended up ruling.

In Greek mythology, as in many others, the world began with darkness. There was nothing but a void, and then, in that void, there was Nyx, goddess of the night and the darkness. Nyx was depicted as a great black bird with wings, and she eventually laid a golden egg. When the egg finally hatched, it split into two parts: one half became the sky, Uranus, and the other became the earth, Gaia.

There are different versions of the creation myth. Some say that there was no bird Nyx and that she came long after the creation of the world, and that at first there was only Chaos, until the mother earth, Gaia, was created. Gaia both gave birth to and married Uranus (also spelled as Ouranos), the sky.

However exactly the earth and the heavens came to be, all Greek mythology agrees that Gaia and Uranus then created the Titans. The Titans were the first children and are generally depicted as dangerous. They're described as both powerful and highly intelligent. One well-known Titan is Prometheus, who gave fire to man against Zeus's wishes and, as punishment, was chained to a rock with an eagle forever plucking out his liver. Another Titan is Atlas, who is forced to hold up the sky with his great strength.

The Titans are also shown to be ruthless and bloodthirsty. They're a representation of barbarous man and the wild tribes that came before the settling of Greek civilization. The next generation, the gods of Olympus, are depicted then to reflect the Greek civilization as it was later on, settled, sophisticated, and civilized. The Titans weren't seen as something to be worshipped by the Greeks, and in fact, there were many fears that the Titans would rise up and come back to take over once again—a metaphor for the idea of barbarism taking over civilization and everything descending into chaos.

The creation myth follows that the youngest titan and the god of time, Cronus, married another titan, Rhea. Cronus rose up and deposed his father Uranus, taking over as the leader of the Titans. He lived in fear that one of his children would do the same, and so every time Rhea gave birth to a child, he would swallow it whole.

They had five children this way, but when the sixth, Zeus, was born, Rhea hid him and instead gave Cronus a rock swaddled in baby clothes, which he swallowed instead. Meanwhile, Rhea hid Zeus in a cave in Crete, where he lived until he was an adult. He then returned to Olympus, the home of the titans, and overthrew his father. He forced his father to disgorge his five other children: Hera, Poseidon, Demeter, Hades, and Hestia. Together, the six of them fought and overthrew the Titans.

The Titans were then banished, and Zeus declared himself the new king of the gods and of man. He then divided up the world between himself and his brothers. Since he had led the gods to victory, he decided he wanted to take the sky, and that would be his dominion. His brother, Poseidon, took charge of the oceans. Hades took charge of the underworld and all below the earth.

A creation myth is basically a myth that in some way explains the origins of something. This Greek creation myth explained to the Greeks the hierarchy of the gods and which god ruled over which area of the earth, so that they knew who to pray to. It also talked about the idea of revolution and of new civilizations overthrowing the old, something that was common in Ancient Greece. Greece operated as a grouping of city-states, including Athens and Sparta, and those city-states were almost constantly at war with one another. The Greeks also highly valued intelligent thinking such as in their study of mathematics, and in fact connected the idea of studying numbers to religion. To study geometry was considered a holy pursuit. In overthrowing the brutish titans, the gods of Olympus represented the enlightened, civilized generation of Greeks and who they strove to be.

Myths that don't deal specifically with the creation of the world can still be dubbed creation myths so long as they explain the origin of something. For example, you've probably heard the phrase "Pandora's box." This comes from the myth where the gods gifted mankind with a few treasures, including a beautiful woman named Pandora. Some say that she was the first woman. Until that point, life had been carefree for mankind. But one of the gifts given to man was a small box. All were instructed not to open it, but Pandora couldn't help herself. She opened it, and out spilled all of the horrid things that we experience in the world today, such as greed, despair, and death. But there was one thing at the bottom of the box, a tiny shimmering light known as Hope. Hope begged Pandora to let it out so that no matter how many horrible things plagued man, they would continue to find the strength to go on.

This counts as a creation myth because it was a way for the Greeks to explain how awful things and emotions had entered the world. We still like to call something a 'Pandora's box' if we know that we shouldn't do it, but it's too tempting not to.

There are many creation myths out there, all of which deal with the idea of figuring out how something came to be. The Greeks pursued scientific studies as well, but they didn't have all the answers and they didn't even always have the equipment necessary to figure out the answers.

To explain why the wind blows, or how stars came to be in the night sky, and so forth, they made creation myths. From those creation myths, the gods and heroes that were created in them were taken and used to make more stories.

Before long, an entire pantheon was born.

Chapter 2: The Gods

A pantheon is a collection of gods and goddesses in those religions that have multiple gods. This is also known as a polytheistic religion. A religion that has only one God, such as Christianity or Islam, is known as a monotheistic religion.

This came about because it made sense to ancient civilizations that each god would have one or two powers and responsibilities so that the work was divided evenly, just like how in an office each person has a few specific responsibilities and the work is divided as evenly as possible so that nobody is overwhelmed. In fact, this idea persists today in monotheistic religions as well. In Catholicism, different saints and angels have domain over different things and so you pray to different ones depending upon what you want. If you're worried about your dog, you would pray to St. Francis of Assisi, who is the patron saint of animals. Islam and Judaism have angels that serve the same purpose. Hinduism is also a monotheistic religion but is often mistaken for a polytheistic one because they divide their one god into multiple facets. That is, multiple gods who each represent one or two traits or domains of the one all-powerful god.

The innate human desire to worship multiple gods and to subdivide tasks is a fascinating one. In Greek religion, this resulted in multiple gods and goddesses. There were multiple gods, but the twelve main gods of Olympus were considered the most powerful. These were Zeus, Hera, Poseidon, Hephaestus, Apollo, Athena, Hermes, Ares, Demeter, Artemis, Aphrodite, and either Dionysus or Hestia—sources differ on this last issue.

The goddesses were just as powerful as the gods and will be detailed in the next chapter, but this chapter will detail the many gods of Greek mythology. One interesting trait that most of them share is that the gods of Greek mythology are the troublemakers. They're the ones who accidentally create monsters, spawn wars, meddle to the detriment of humanity, and so on.

Zeus

Let's take the first god, the king of the other gods, Zeus. Zeus is the god of the sky and thunder, and is in charge of the other gods, assigning them their roles and acting as a judge over any disputes.

However, Zeus also causes a lot of trouble for the gods, since he is depicted in mythology as famously lustful. He fathered more gods and heroes than any other god, and most stories involving him have him chasing after a woman, a goddess, or a nature spirit such as a dyad or naiad.

The majority of the heroes featured in Greek mythology are the offspring of Zeus. Helen, the princess who, when captured, started the Trojan War, is Zeus's daughter. Her mother tried to get away from Zeus by turning herself into a goose, but he turned himself into a swan and followed her. She laid a few eggs, all of which became human children, and the most beautiful of them was Helen.

Athena is another one of Zeus's children, having sprung fully formed out of his head after he drank her mother Metis, the goddess of wisdom, in an effort to prevent a child being born. Twin gods Apollo and Artemis, Hermes, Dionysus, Nemesis, the three Fates, and the nine Muses are all Zeus's children. With his wife Hera he had three god children: Ares, Hebe, and Hephaestus. And then with the goddess Demeter, he had Persephone, the goddess of spring.

Some of the heroes that Zeus fathered include Heracles (better known by the Roman spelling of his name, Hercules) and the hero Perseus. He also fathered the king Minos, a powerful figure in mythology, and the king Tantalus, who became a tyrant and was punished in the underworld. He also fathered various monsters as a result of turning himself into animals in order to get close to the mortal women he wanted to sleep with. He slept with Europa as a bull and so she gave birth to the Minotaur, and he slept with Selene as a lion and so the Nemean Lion was born.

Zeus's conquests often caused trouble. Sometimes this was because his wife, Hera, the goddess of marriage, was angry at his infidelity and would punish his children or girlfriends because she was unable to punish Zeus himself. Other times, this was because his children would be too powerful, or would be monsters, and so would cause destruction. This would leave Zeus needing to send one of the other gods or a hero to deal with the situation. And if a woman refused him, he found a way to punish her. Aphrodite, for instance, refused him, and as punishment, he married her to Hephaestus, the ugliest of the gods.

However, despite his flaws, Zeus was believed to be the most powerful of the gods, and a just ruler. The Olympic games were held in his honor and he had the biggest feasts and the most worshippers. He is one of the most prominent figures in Greek mythology, and the idea of a powerful, bearded, all-father type character persists today, including in our depictions of a Christian God.

Poseidon

The god of the ocean and earthquakes, as well as horses, Poseidon did not feature in as many stories as Zeus did. However, he was the chief god worshipped in the city-states of Thebes and Pylos, and a few myths talk of his anger. Odysseus, the titular character of the Odyssey, angers Poseidon, and in retaliation, Poseidon keeps him lost at sea for ten years before he is able to return home. Despite his anger against Odysseus, Poseidon is on the side of the Greeks in the famous Trojan War, and is depicted as often assisting them.

While Poseidon did not have as many affairs as Zeus did, he had one famous affair that resulted in one of Greek mythology's most enduring monsters. Poseidon and Athena had a long-standing rivalry after the city of Athens was created. The people were unsure which god to name their city after. Poseidon gave them a well of water, while Athena gifted them an olive tree. At first, the people were joyful for the water, but then they realized that it was saltwater, and was therefore, undrinkable. So they chose to name their city after Athena, for olive oil was used to cook food, light lanterns, and bathe, and the wood from the tree was used for fire. Thus, the city of Athens was named.

The bitter rivalry continued for some time, until one day Poseidon pursued and raped Medusa, a beautiful woman, on the floor of one of Athena's temples. Athena then turned Medusa into a hideous Gorgon and gave her the power to turn men to stone. Whether this was done to punish Medusa or to save her from being approached by any man ever again is uncertain, but Medusa became one of the most well-known monsters in Greek mythology. Medusa also bore two of Poseidon's children, Pegasus and the giant Chrysaor.

Poseidon also had an affair with a mortal woman leading to the birth of Theseus, who defeated the famed Minotaur and escaped his labyrinth. He also sired the race of Cyclops, the giants with only one eye. As the father of earthquakes, which the ancient Greeks believed was caused by the ocean waves eroding rocks on the sea floor, he was also believed to be the cause of epilepsy, an "earthquake" of the human body. His most famous offspring was Bellerophon, considered one of the greatest heroes of mythology, who slayed the famous Chimera.

Hades

The god of the underworld, Hades is often depicted as a villain, since modern civilization tends to see death as something scary and monstrous. However, in ancient Greek times, Hades was a good character and was known as the most impartial and just of the gods. The underworld was, to the Greeks, not something to fear, and many myths feature heroes going into the underworld for one purpose or another.

Hades generally treats these heroes well as long as they mean him no harm, but he also abides by the rules of the underworld and does not let anyone simply cheat death. He oversees the torture and punishment of wrongdoers, such as Tantalus, who served his own children to the gods. As punishment, Tantalus stands at a river, eternally hungry and thirsty, with the water just out of his reach and the fruit of a tree just out of his grasp. This is, incidentally, where our word "tantalizing" comes from.

Various stories depict heroes dealing with Hades, and he is never shown to be angry, but rather, stern. He allows Heracles to borrow his guard dog, Cerberus, so long as Heracles returns him, and he lets the hero Theseus go after paralyzing Theseus for a time when Theseus tried to steal Hades' wife. He also allows Orpheus to take back his wife after Orpheus plays music for him, so long as Orpheus does not look back to make sure she is still there (an allegory on trusting one another, since Orpheus does indeed look back, not trusting that his wife is following him, and so loses her for good).

In fact, Hades is the only god who does not take consorts. He has his wife, Persephone, and remains loyal to her. The myth of Persephone is an enduring one and was created not only as an explanation for why we have winter, but also as a metaphor for the journey of a woman from a girl to an adult, leaving her childhood home for her husband's.

Forgotten by most is that Hades is also the god of wealth, since precious metals and gems came from beneath the earth, and therefore were thought to come from the underworld.

Apollo

One of the twin gods, Apollo is the son of Zeus, the brother of Artemis, and the god of the sun, medicine, archery, music, poetry, art, and the oracles. All oracles, or those who were believed to see into the future, were said to be blessed by Apollo and held him as their patron.

Apollo was very similar to his father in that he had many consorts and was known for punishing women who did not wish to sleep with him. In one famous myth, he pursues Diana, a nymph, who turns into a tree in order to save herself from being taken by him. When he pursued Cassandra, a prophet, and she rejected him, he cursed her so that nobody would ever believe anything that she said—and so her prophecies about the destruction of Troy fell on deaf ears.

Various art competitions, especially poetry and music, were held in his name, with large prizes for the winners. Apollo was thought to be the leader of the Muses, the goddesses who gave mankind inspiration to perform various arts such as painting and theatre.

Apollo was on the side of the Trojans in the Trojan War, and his behavior is what lead to the anger of Achilles, one of the heroes, which in turn caused the events of the Iliad. He is the god that assists Paris in letting loose the arrow that kills Achilles. He is also believed to be the father of Orpheus, Greek mythology's most renowned singer/poet.

Hermes

A child of Zeus and the second-youngest of the Olympian gods, Hermes serves as their messenger, and is a sort of jack-of-all-trades god. He is the god of trade, travelers, sports, athletes, border crossings, thieves, and doctors, with his caduceus being the widely-recognized symbol for medicine. He is also the guide to the Underworld when a person dies.

Hermes is a very playful god and is often shown performing tricks or pranks on other gods, sometimes with the help of Aphrodite, his partner in crime, and sometimes lover. He uses his winged sandals to fly, and although he is a trickster god, he is also the god that is most often on the side of humanity. Many of his tricks are on the gods in order to benefit humans.

Hermes was the god that seemed most sympathetic to humanity, shown in how he protected Priam in the Trojan War, despite Priam being on the Trojan side, the side that Hermes opposed. Priam snuck into the Greek camp to obtain the body of his son Hector for burial, and Hermes granted him good luck and invisibility so that he succeeded and was able to bury his son properly.

Hermes did not have many offspring, but his two most well-known were Pan and Autolycus. He also possibly fathered Perseus, depending upon the myth. Autolycus was known as the prince of thieves and was the grandfather of Odysseus, while Pan is a famous demigod and the ruler of the wild places in the world.

Ares

The god of war, Ares, was a contrast to Athena, the goddess of war, in that he was the unchecked rage and bloodlust of war; the darker, less honorable sides of it. Ares was famous for his temper and created two sons, Phobos (Fear) and Deimos (Terror), who, along with his lover Enyo (Discord), accompanied him in battle.

Most of the Greeks were rather ambivalent towards Ares. They saw him as embodying the necessary and unavoidable parts of war, and at his best, he represented the valor and courage that came out in warriors. Most soldiers and warriors would pray to him in battle for victory, but more out of fear of angering him and having him be on the opposite side, than any real love for him.

The most famous myth featuring Ares is actually about his lover Aphrodite, the goddess of love. Ares would often sneak into the home of Hephaestus, Aphrodite's husband, to sleep with her while Hephaestus was away. One time, Hephaestus set a trap for them with a golden net that kept them captive, and the lovers were laughed at by all of the other gods. Most myths involving Ares actually tend to deal with his humiliation, suggesting that the idea of the macho man was not embraced by ancient Greeks. In fact, intelligence and learning were more highly valued than just fighting prowess, and it was expected that men should also be able to discuss philosophy, mathematics, and even art as well as fight in battle. To be just a brute, so to speak, was laughable, and so Ares is often laughed at in mythology.

Hephaestus

The son of Zeus and Hera, Hephaestus was the god of fire, metalworking, forging, and the art of sculpting and blacksmithing. He was the patron of these arts and made all of the weapons for the gods, including Zeus's lightning bolts. He was a clever and honorable god but was said to be horribly ugly because, during a fight between Zeus and Hera, Hephaestus stepped in between to protect his mother. Zeus flung him out the window in anger, casting him onto the ground, but Olympus was so high up that it took him days to fall. When he did land, it horribly disfigured him.

In another version of the myth, however, it is Hera who tosses Hephaestus out the window because he was born disfigured and she hated the sight of him. In this version, Zeus rescues him and places him inside a volcano where he can forge to his heart's content.

Hephaestus is married to Aphrodite, the goddess of love, but this union makes both unhappy and was done by Zeus in order to punish Aphrodite for refusing him. Aphrodite has numerous affairs, but Hephaestus only punishes her for her affair with Ares, suggesting that it is not so much her affairs, as Ares himself, that he objects to. This could further represent the metaphor of what the ancient Greeks valued, since Hephaestus represented skill, artistry, wisdom, and was said to have healing powers, and therefore humiliated Ares, the man who represents unbridled anger and brute strength.

While there are several conflicting myths and not much can be said definitively, most scholars agree with sources that say that Hephaestus was in love with Athena, and often pursued her. Whether he succeeded in wooing her or if Athena was open to the idea is unknown.

Dionysus

The youngest of the Greek gods, Dionysus was born of Zeus and Semele, a human princess. Dionysus is the god of revelry, wine, theatre, fertility, and religious ecstasy. A person who has gone crazy is said to have been touched by the madness of Dionysus.

Like Hades, Dionysus has a wife that he is said to adore, although unlike Hades, Dionysus has other children by other women. Ariadne, his wife, was a mortal woman who assisted the human hero Theseus in defeating the Minotaur. Theseus sailed away with her, but then abandoned her on an island. Seeing her distress, Dionysus came to her and proposed marriage. Ariadne accepted and was made immortal and taken to Olympus. Despite his affairs, many poems speak of his devotion and love for Ariadne, and she never seemed to seek revenge on Dionysus or his lovers the way other goddess-wives such as Hera did.

While Dionysus was not one of the most important or powerful gods in terms of what he had control over, he quickly became one of the most popular. Theatre as we know it today originally started as a kind of celebratory dance in Dionysus's honor, and he had many festivals in his name. His story of birth, death, and rebirth, said to be similar to that of Jesus Christ in Christianity, was wildly popular and re-enacted every year by actors and accompanied by sacrifices.

Wild parties were usually attributed to Dionysus, and he was often given as an excuse for drunken, disorderly behavior. He even had groups of wild followers who would live in the hills and wreak havoc. His residing over parties and wild times was most likely what contributed to his popularity, especially since wine was such an important product and export for Greece.

Chapter 3: The Goddesses

Goddesses in Greek mythology were generally more responsible and often more warrior-like than the gods. While the gods were powerful, the goddesses were the ones to actively fear the wrath of, and the stories of goddesses taking revenge are more well-known and numerous than the ones about the gods.

Hera

The queen of the gods and the wife of Zeus, Hera was the goddess of the family and mothers. She was prayed to when a woman was in labor and if a child was sick and was said to protect the family bond. She was also asked to bless marriages.

Hera is most known, however, for her jealous behavior regarding her husband. Zeus was the most prolific of the gods, having countless affairs and children, and Hera would often take revenge on the women and their children since she couldn't attack Zeus himself. She plucked out the eyes of Io, one of Zeus's lovers, and chased Leto, the mother of Apollo and Artemis, around the world so that she could not stop and give birth to them. Many women avoided, or tried to avoid, sex with Zeus so that they would not be attacked by Hera afterwards.

Despite her mostly being known for this, Hera was a staple in Greek households. She didn't have many feast days and wasn't popular in the way of Athena or Dionysus, but she was a quiet presence that was incorporated into the home and daily activities, such as prayers from mothers, or a small shrine in the house. She was incorporated into childbirth rituals and marriage ceremonies, and was a quiet but constant part of daily life in Ancient Greece.

Athena

Arguably the most popular goddess, if not the most popular of all the gods no matter their gender, Athena was the goddess of war, wisdom, and handicraft. She was the patron god of Athens and had numerous feast days, and was said to guide heroes in battle. Athena represented the intelligence and military stratagem of war and was the honorable, heroic side of it, as opposed to Ares who represented the bloodthirstiness and violence.

Athena features often in mythology, and can be shown as merciful, just, or vengeful, depending upon the myth. The one thing that she does not like is being shown up, although all of the gods dislike this. For example, when Arachne, a young weaver, boasted that she was better than Athena, Athena challenged her to a weaving competition. Arachne then wove a tapestry depicting the gods as drunken idiots. Angered by the disrespect, Athena turned her into a spider, which is where we get the term "arachnid."

Gods and goddesses often have unusual beginnings, and Athena was no exception. She was said to have been born when her father, Zeus, slept with Metis, the goddess of wisdom and knowledge. He then heard that the child of himself and Metis would have a child more powerful than Zeus himself. To prevent this, Zeus tricked Metis into turning herself into a fly and swallowed her. But Metis was already pregnant, and Athena grew out of Zeus's head. When his headache was too great, he begged Hephaestus to split his head open with his great hammer. This was done and out popped Athena, fully grown and wearing her distinctive armor.

While she was a virgin goddess who had no children of her own, she was a patron and mentor to many heroes, including Perseus, Heracles, Bellerophon, Odysseus, and Jason. She is one of the three goddesses who fought over the golden apple that started the Trojan War, and supported the Greeks during the war.

In one myth, Athena also has an adoptive son named Erichthonius. The story runs that Hephaestus tried to rape her, and Athena managed to fight him off. Hephaestus instead had his seed fall to the earth, the earth being the goddess Gaia. Gaia got pregnant and gave birth to Erichtonius. Feeling bad for the poor child, Athena took him in and raised him.

Athena's popularity continued into the Renaissance period, where she came to represent a classical education and learning, and was a symbol for freedom and democracy.

Artemis

The twin of Apollo and the daughter of Zeus and Leto, Artemis was the chaste goddess of the hunt, who led a group of women in eternal hunts through the forests. She was also the goddess of the moon, stags, and dogs. Some scholars debate that she was not chaste, but rather only a lover of women.

Only Orion, a great hunter, ever won Artemis's heart, but before they could be together, he was accidentally murdered by her in a trick by her brother Apollo. Artemis never forgave Apollo for it, and she turned Orion into a constellation so that he would be forever remembered.

When Artemis and Apollo were born, it is said that Artemis was born first, while her mother Leto was still being pursued by monsters sent by Hera. Artemis fought them off and protected her mother so that Leto could give birth to Apollo. While Artemis and her brother were gods and could not be easily killed, she, her brother, and Hera had a very cool relationship, without warmth, and were often shown on opposite sides of an argument.

Multiple men in mythology lust after and try to obtain Artemis. Unlike many other myths, however, where the woman must sacrifice something or transform in order to escape and the man never experiences consequences, Artemis repeatedly kills or otherwise punishes the men who attempt to rape her.

Artemis was also involved in the Trojan War. Agamemnon, the leader of the Greek forces and brother-in-law to Helen of Troy, was unable to get his warships to leave the harbor because he insulted Artemis and said he was a better hunter than she was. As penance, he sacrificed his youngest and favorite child, Iphigenia. At the moment of her death, Artemis spirited her away and made her one of her immortal hunting companions. Agamemnon's willingness to sacrifice his daughter broke the curse Artemis placed upon him, and he was able to sail to Troy to bring Helen back.

Her rivalry with Hera also came to a head during the Trojan War, where Hera was on the side of the Greeks, and Artemis was on the side of the Trojans in support of her brother Apollo. The two goddesses actually came to blows and Zeus had to intervene.

Artemis was worshipped by both men and women, men for her hunting prowess and women for her chastity and protection of young girls. She didn't have many feast days, but was considered one of the most "human" of the gods who actively participated and interacted with humanity. She was also a symbol for daughters, since she consistently protected her mother and sought her council.

Demeter

The goddess of agriculture, harvest, fertility, and sacred law or oaths, Demeter was the one most worshipped by farmers in the hopes that they would have a successful crop that year. Despite her powers over the earth, she is most known for the story involving her daughter, Persephone, which is how she came to be worshipped as an enforcer of oaths and promises.

Demeter originally had some of the most influence and power in the mythology because of Greece's status as farmers. However, as Greece grew in military power and turned more towards war and scientific discovery, Demeter's influence waned. She was said to generally side with Poseidon against Zeus.

Despite this, she had one child with Zeus, Persephone. She had other children, but Persephone was her pride and joy, and also the only one who was immortal. One day while Persephone was out, she was taken by Hades to be his bride. Demeter was furious and demanded her daughter back. When Hades refused, she turned the world barren. Cold winds came, and nothing grew.

The other gods begged Demeter to give the earth back its fertility, but she refused until her daughter was returned to her. Hades and Persephone, however, refused.

Zeus finally intervened and decreed that Persephone would spend nine months out of the year with her mother, and three months with her husband. The three months when Persephone is with Hades, Demeter has the ground wither, which is how the Greeks explained where winter came from. The demand that Persephone and Hades honor the bonds of motherhood and adhere to Zeus's oath are where Demeter gets her dominion over laws and oaths from.

Hestia

The goddess of the hearth and home, Hestia is often forgotten. In fact, many people would replace her with the more popular Dionysus in the twelve gods of Olympus lineup.

Hestia represents order, so she was worshipped not just when it came to the home, but also the state, and even architecture since all buildings had to be properly in order or they would fall down. The center of each city had a sacred flame dedicated to Hestia that would burn eternally, and when a new city was established, a part of that flame would be carried to the new city and stationed there. This was because the heart of a home was the hearth, or fire pit, and so the center of the city had to have a hearth as well because a city-state was merely a larger version of a family, and both had to be orderly.

Interestingly, Hestia is actually the oldest of the Olympian gods, since she is the first child of Cronus and Rhea. This could be because she represents the foundations of the family and the city-state, and that order and value came before all else. Therefore, the goddess who represented it had to come before all the others, even if she was not always the most celebrated.

Despite not being the most celebrated, every time a sacrifice was made to the gods, a small portion of it 'went to Hestia first' because the home and family were never to be forgotten. While she never took a vow of chastity like Artemis or Athena, Hestia is not recorded as having any spouse or children, and is dedicated to humanity as her family. The gentlest and most passive of the gods, Hestia is not often thought of in modern times, but she was possibly the most valued and fundamental god in the eyes of the ancient Greeks.

Aphrodite

While she is one of the twelve gods of Olympus, Aphrodite has unusual origins. When the god Uranus was slain, his blood fell into the sea, stirring up foam. From that foam was born Aphrodite. She is the goddess of beauty, love, pleasure, and sexuality. She is most famous for being a representation and pinnacle of female beauty in western culture. She is also often invoked by poets when they are in love or when they wish to praise their mortal lovers' beauty.

Aphrodite was originally sought by Zeus, but she rebuffed him. As punishment, she was married to Hephaestus, a misshapen god whom she did not love. Aphrodite was repeatedly unfaithful to him, most notably with Ares, the god of war. She was also the cohort and sometimes lover of Hermes.

While Aphrodite had many lovers, one of her most well-known is Adonis. As a child, Adonis was raised by Persephone as her son, but he became the most beautiful of men and Aphrodite wanted him. The two women fought over him, and Zeus decreed that Adonis would get to spend a third of the year with Persephone, a third of the year with Aphrodite, and a third of the year however he chose. Adonis chose to spend that third with Aphrodite as well, until he was gored by a wild boar and sent to the Underworld permanently. Adonis became a symbol of handsome young men (so a young man who is good looking is said to be 'an Adonis'), and he is the most well-known of Aphrodite's lovers—however, she had no children with him.

She did have children with her other lovers, the most famous being Eros, her son by Ares. Eros was the god of love, and is where we get our modern idea of Cupid. Eros had a pack of arrows and would fire them into people's hearts to get them to fall in love. Unfortunately, the gods often commanded him to use this ability to manipulate mortals.

A famous myth details how Eros fell in love with Psyche, a woman even more beautiful than Aphrodite. Aphrodite hated Psyche for this and tried to kill her, but failed, and Psyche was eventually married to Eros and made immortal.

Aphrodite also had another mortal lover, Anchises, a man of Troy. Their son, Aeneas, was said to go on to Italy and become the father of the Romans. His story is detailed in the Roman epic, the Aeneid, which tells of the events that followed the Trojan War from the perspective of the Trojans (where The Odyssey tells the story from the perspective of the Greeks).

Aphrodite was famous for heavily rewarding those that honored her and brutally punishing those that angered her. This is possibly why Paris chose to give her the golden apple in the events that led to the Trojan War, despite angering Artemis and Hera with this choice. She was especially fond of causing men's horses to tear them apart and eat them.

Throughout history and into the present day, Aphrodite is one of the most popular goddesses. A version of her can be found in most mythologies, and she is said to be an updated version of the goddess Ishtar from Mesopotamian mythology. Many present-day pagan religions such as Wicca still worship her.

Persephone

One of the youngest gods, Persephone is the daughter of Demeter and Zeus. Her original name was actually Kore, meaning maiden, and she was the goddess of spring and innocence. After she married Hades, she became the goddess of the underworld and is said to have been majestic, intimidating, and the one who decided and carried out the punishment for wrongdoers. She was the one to fear in the Underworld, rather than her husband. In fact, in the Underworld, it was forbidden to even speak her name.

This myth of going from girlhood innocence to a powerful woman in charge is allegorical for the journey a woman was supposed to make in society from a child to an adult, moving from the house of her mother to the home of her husband, and carrying out her duties as head of the household and master of the servants. Persephone was a popular goddess who had an entire cult dedicated to her.

The myth of Persephone's abduction by and marriage to Hades has various versions. The most basic is that Hades captured her and then tricked her into eating some pomegranate seeds so that she had to spend part of the year in the Underworld with him. However, other sources say that Zeus lusted after Persephone and she agreed to marry Hades, eating the seeds willingly so that she could spend part of the year with him.

This second interpretation is given credence by the fact that Persephone never takes any other lovers and has no children, while other unwillingly married goddesses such as Aphrodite have numerous affairs. Persephone does, however, adopt Adonis as her child after his mother is turned into a tree.

There were many other gods, such as Nike, the goddess of athletes and victory, and Morpheus, the god of dreams, but these were the main gods and goddesses who were worshipped by the people of Greece and most often invoked in their mythologies.

Chapter 4: Heroes And Monsters

The gods often starred in myths, but more often they were the secondary characters, assisting or hindering the mortals who rose above the common man to become something more: the heroes. Enduring throughout time, these characters are still invoked today, known for their power in battle, their cunning, and their courage. And on the other side, were the ones who opposed them and brought terror to the land—the monsters they slew.

Jason

Unlike many heroes, Jason was completely mortal. He was the son of a king, Aeson, and a mother, although the identity of his mother changes depending upon various myths.

While he was just a baby, his elder half-brother slew their father Aeson and took his throne. Their mother, terrified for her son, had her handmaidens gather around the baby and cry as if he were stillborn. She then spirited him away to Chiron, a centaur and trainer of heroes, to be raised. When he was an adult, Jason returned to his home city to fight his half-brother for the throne. His half-brother told him that he could claim the throne when he brought back the fabled Golden Fleece, and Jason agreed, wanting to avoid war.

Jason then assembled a group of heroes, known as the Argonauts, and set off. Hercules and Orpheus, two other important heroes, were a part of this group. They had many adventures along the way but eventually came to the island where the fleece was held and guarded by a dragon. The local king agreed to give the fleece to Jason if he successfully performed three tasks. Hera persuaded Eros to make the king's daughter, Medea, fall in love with him and assist him. Jason was successful with her magical help, and they fled together, but Jason then abandoned her, fearing her magical powers.

Because he abandoned Medea and broke his promise to her, he lost favor with Hera, goddess of marriage. He died lonely and unhappy when the stern of the rotting Argo, his ship, fell on him.

Orpheus

The supposed son of Apollo and a mortal woman, Orpheus is one of the few heroes not known for his fighting skills. Rather, he was a skilled musician and poet, said to be the best in the land. Other myths say that he is the son of one of the Muses, Calliope, and a mortal king.

Orpheus, like many mythological characters, might have actually been a historical figure. There are fragments of poetry attributed to him that survive today, and other accounts given that list many more epics (long, poem-formatted stories) by him that were lost to time.

The myth of Orpheus that is the most enduring is the story of his lost wife, Eurydice. The myth goes that Eurydice died, some say bitten by a snake, and Orpheus was so heartbroken that he was determined to go to the Underworld and get her back. He made it past the giant three-headed guard dog Cerberus by playing music that made him fall asleep. He then played music for Persephone and Hades. Swayed by his skill, they agreed to give him back Eurydice, but he must prove his trust in her by walking out of the Underworld without once looking behind him, trusting that she would be following.

Orpheus had just reached the entrance to the Underworld and was almost home when he gave into temptation and looked back. He had just enough time to see that Eurydice had in fact been following him the entire time and was faithful, before she vanished, gone forever since he had failed the test. Orpheus then allowed himself to be torn apart by wild women who worshipped Dionysus so that he could die and join Eurydice in the underworld permanently.

However, Orpheus was involved in other myths, including as a member of the Argonauts with Jason.

Theseus

The king and founder of the city of Athens, Theseus was the son of the mortal king Aegeus and the daughter of Aegeus's friend and fellow king Pittheus, known as Aethra. After Aethra and Aegeus slept together, Aethra had a dream from Athena that told her to go into the ocean. She did so and was possessed by Poseidon, who gave her child some of his power. Thus, Theseus was technically a demigod despite having two mortal parents.

Theseus was raised by his mother, and told of his true parentage only as an adult. He then set out to find his father, encountering six entrances to the Underworld along the way and having to defeat the guardians at each entrance.

When he reached Athens, he learned from his father that they were in the middle of an awful grief. Athens had lost a great war to Crete, and as a sacrifice, they now had to send six young women and six young men to Crete every few years, where they would be given to the Minotaur in his labyrinth. Theseus volunteered to join them and slay the monster.

He journeyed to Crete, where he met King Minos and his daughter Ariadne. Ariadne fell in love with Theseus and gave him a ball of thread so that he could find his way out of the labyrinth. She was also able to smuggle him a sword. She even gave him instructions to find the center of the maze where the Minotaur was. Theseus slew the Minotaur and came back out of the maze, where he and the other Athenian youths fled with Ariadne back to Athens. Along the way, for reasons unknown, he abandoned Ariadne.

Theseus's victory was marred by grief, however, for he had promised his father that if he survived he would change the ship's black sails to white. He forgot this, and so when his father saw the black sails, he thought that his son had died and threw himself off a cliff, committing suicide.

Perseus

Another demigod, Perseus is the child of Zeus and the mortal woman Danae. His grandfather heard from an oracle that his grandson would kill him, and so locked Danae up in a chamber that was open only to the sky. Zeus came down to her in the form of golden sunlight. His grandfather was scared of his grandson but couldn't kill the child of Zeus, so he sent Danae and the infant Perseus out to sea in a wooden chest. They were found by a fisherman who took them in. The local king wanted to marry Danae, but Perseus protected his mother, and the king contrived to have Perseus sent away in disgrace.

The king plotted to have a feast where each person must gift him with a horse, supposedly so he could win the hand of a princess who was known for taming horses. Perseus had no horse, and so instead asked for the king to name another gift that Perseus could give him—Perseus would not refuse him. Taking advantage of this rash promise, the king told Perseus to bring him the head of Medusa.

One of the most enduring monsters of Greek mythology, Medusa was cursed by Athena so that she would have tusks, wings, goggling eyes, snakes for hair, and so that her gaze would turn anything that met it to stone.

Luckily, Athena aided Perseus and gifted him, among other things, a shield that was shiny enough to be a mirror. Perseus looked in the mirror, rather than at Medusa, so that he could see her and fight her without being turned to stone. He cut off her head and returned to the king and used Medusa's head on him, so that he was turned to stone.

Perseus did, in fact, kill his grandfather, but by accident. He was traveling and competing in a discus throwing competition that his grandfather was attending—ironically, so that he would not be at home, for he had heard of Perseus returning. The disc went wild and struck him in the head, killing him.

This is another recurring theme in Greek mythology: that the more you struggle against prophecy and the gods, the more you actually set events in line for it to happen.

Bellerophon

Considered the greatest hero (along with Cadmus and Perseus) before Hercules, one of Bellerophon's greatest acts of heroism was slaying the Chimera.

The Chimera is a popular monster in Greek mythology. It employs the traditional mythological concept of combining various animals into one hideous monster. In this case, the chimera had the head of a lion, a goat, and a dragon, the body of a lion, and the tail of a snake. Nowadays, any creature of fiction that is made by combining the parts of different animals is called a "chimera" creature.

Bellerophon was the son of a mortal woman and Poseidon, although some say he was fully mortal and the son of the woman's husband. He captured Pegasus, the flying horse, and used him to fly above the chimera and drop lead down its throat. When the chimera breathed fire again it melted the lead, which suffocated it and killed it. It's said that the "eternal fires" in Lycia (modern-day Turkey) are left over from the chimera's death throes.

However, eventually Bellerophon became too proud of himself and tried to fly all the way up to Olympus, feeling he was the equal of the gods. Zeus sent a fly to bite Pegasus, so he accidentally bucked Bellerophon off, causing him to fall. The story of a person growing too proud and angering the gods as a result is another tenant of Greek mythology.

Cadmus

The founder of Thebes, Cadmus was said to have invented the phonetic alphabet, and was known as one of the greatest heroes before the arrival of Hercules. He killed a water dragon and other creatures during his quest to find and rescue his sister Europa, who had been kidnapped by Zeus in the form of a bull.

Cadmus's heroism was such that the gods allowed him to marry Harmonia, the goddess of harmony, who was the daughter of Aphrodite and Ares.

Dragons, in Ancient Greece, were not considered the intelligent creatures that we often now think of them as. Modern times often like to paint dragons as sources of wisdom and magic, but in ancient times, dragons were viewed as simply another kind of animal, albeit one that was more dangerous and could breathe fire. There are several accounts of dragons in mythology, including Cadmus's exploits, but none of the dragons can talk—although they are cunning creatures and oftentimes magic or quick thinking must be used to defeat them rather than simply brute force.

Hercules

The greatest hero of them all, Hercules—or Heracles in the proper Greek spelling, although the Roman name for him is the one that we all know—was the son of Zeus and the mortal Alcmene. He was, interestingly, both the great-grandson and half-brother of Perseus. Alcmene was descended from Perseus, but Hercules's father was Zeus, who was also Perseus's father.

Ancient Greek mythology could often be confusing in this way, since all the gods are in some way related and were also marrying or having relations with one another and various mortals, who were also often related since most mortals who became heroes and interacted with the gods were royalty in some way.

Hercules spent much of his life struggling against the machinations of Hera, who hated him as she hated all of Zeus's illegitimate children—but Hercules was known especially for his heroism, consistently reminded people that he was a son of Zeus with his physical strength. The most famous incident was when Hera caused Hercules to go mad, killing his wife Megara and his children. When Hercules recovered from his manic fit, he consulted an oracle on how to atone, but the oracle was secretly Hera and she told him he must serve his cousin and perform the labors the cousin asked of him. The subsequent Twelve Labors of Hercules are his most famous works.

These labors involved dealing with flesh-eating horses, the Hydra, and taking Cerberus out of the Underworld. He also had to capture a wild boar and slay the Nemean Lion, a monstrous child of Zeus's. Most of the famous Greek monsters of mythology were dealt with by Hercules—in fact, the deeds of Hercules are about twice that as those done by other heroes. His enduring popularity in Greek mythology, and then subsequently Roman mythology and today's popular culture, is intriguing.

Part of it could well be that Hercules was known not just for his brute strength but for his intelligence, his acts of penance to the gods, and his extreme compassion and generosity towards his friends.

Hercules is arguably the most recognizable character from Greek mythology and has been the subject of multiple films and television shows. Whatever the reasons, he is the ultimate symbol of Greek mythology and ancient heroes.

Chapter 5: Important Myths

We've already covered in various places throughout the book myths that were important to the Greeks, including detailing the actions of their famous heroes. However, there are plenty of other myths that didn't necessarily feature one of the famed heroes, or if they did, the focus was not upon the heroes but upon others. Many are so well-known to us that they are ingrained into our culture without our even knowing it.

For example, someone can have an "Oedipus complex," a diagnosable psychological condition—that phrase comes from the myth of Oedipus. If someone has the "Midas touch," where it seems as though everything they participate in turns out well, that comes from the myth of King Midas.

It can be difficult for historians to catalogue all of the myths, because myths changed over time and could be combined with one another, or told featuring different characters. This chapter will share some of the most famous myths.

Oedipus

This myth actually gained fame because the story was turned into a series of plays about the doomed king Oedipus and his family. The story is also a cautionary tale, warning people of what would happen if they grew too proud and defied the gods, or tried to go against destiny. Everything that people do in the stories to defy the oracle's prophecy actually helps to enable that prophecy to happen.

The prophecy is that the son of the king will kill his father and marry his mother, so the king has a servant take his son into the woods to be devoured by wild animals. The servant leaves the child, but the baby is found by another king and queen. The child grows up to be Oedipus. He travels as a young man and along the way, runs into an older man who is rude to him. He kills him, and then visits the next kingdom. He learns that the king has disappeared, and he and the queen fall in love and get married.

Almost immediately, a plague falls over the land and Oedipus goes to the oracle to learn how to stop it. He learns that the man who killed the previous king must suffer penance, and that the son who married his mother must also do penance. In due time it is revealed that Oedipus is that son, and that the man he killed on the road was the king, his true father. Therefore, the prophecy was fulfilled, and he killed his father and married his mother, not knowing who they were and they not knowing who he was.

Prometheus

This myth deals with the idea of man being given a gift that will enable them to move forward technologically. As the Greeks grew more reliant on science and technology, many said that they would anger the gods for their presumptuousness. This was one of the myths that dealt with that idea.

Prometheus was one of the few titans who was not punished when Zeus took over Olympus, as he was an intelligent person who served Zeus well. But he saw mankind suffering and begged Zeus to allow him to help the humans. Zeus forbade it, but Prometheus secretly gave mankind fire anyway. With fire, mankind was able to progress technologically.

As punishment, Zeus chained Prometheus to a rock, where an eagle would peck out his liver every day, and every day the liver would grow back. This went on for years until Hercules killed the eagle and rescued Prometheus. In return, Prometheus told Hercules several bits of prophecy, for Prometheus had the gift of foresight. Of course, this means that Prometheus knew what would happen to him if he gave mankind fire, and chose to help them anyway despite knowing what punishment awaited him.

The idea of Prometheus is so enduring, that Mary Shelley's full title for her novel Frankenstein is actually Frankenstein: or, the Modern Prometheus.

King Midas

This myth is actually also presented as one of the famous Aesop's Fables, short stories that contain a moral for people to learn from. King Midas was a rich and powerful king who was also greedy and asked to be given the ability to turn everything he touched into gold. Zeus granted his wish. At first, King Midas was delighted by this turn of events. But then his beloved daughter ran to greet him and the moment he touched her, she turned into gold.

King Midas begged Zeus for help. Zeus told him to dip his hands into the water of a certain spring, and then to take that water and sprinkle it on anything he had turned into gold. Midas did so and used it to revive his daughter, and from then on was humble and gave all that he had away.

This story was told in a much more simplistic style than most Greek myths, employing the classic Greek idea that too much pride will lead to someone's downfall. It's also a gentler story than most, as nobody dies or suffers permanently.

Sisyphus

The myth of Sisyphus endures because of the torment that he endures in Tartarus, the section of the Underworld reserved for those who needed to be punished, such as the previously mentioned Tantalus.

Sisyphus was a king and ruler who encouraged trade and established a lot of good for his city but was also known for his ruthlessness. One of the most important rules in Ancient Greece was the idea of hospitality: you were to treat your guests well. Feed them, bathe them, and help them if you could.

Sisyphus would kill his guests and show their bodies off to his subjects to remind them of his ruthlessness. This blatant disregard for the sacred rules of hospitality angered Zeus. He tried to have Sisyphus killed, but was outsmarted by Sisyphus on multiple occasions, until finally he succeeded. Sisyphus's punishment was to push a large boulder up a hill to the top, but each time when he got close to the top, the weight would prove too great and the rock would roll back to the bottom, and so Sisyphus would have to start all over again for eternity.

Nowadays, if someone has a "Sisyphean task," they are doing something that they will never actually get to finish.

These are just a few of the popular myths that were prevalent in Ancient Greece, but many myths had the same themes as these ones: pride will lead to a downfall, treat others well, and don't try to defy the gods.

Chapter 6: Hyacinthus

Hyacinthus (also known as Hyacinth) was a young, handsome Spartan Prince. Hyacinthus was a great friend, and also lover of the god Apollo.

One day, whilst walking upon a hillside, Apollo saw another shepherd boy, who was playing music on a pipe. Apollo was attracted by his music, and headed towards him. As Apollo drew near, he stopped and stood before the shepherd, asking " What is thy name, noble youth?". The shepherd was stunned by the brightness emanating from the god, but responded simply. " Hyacinthus". Apollo then asked Hyacinthus if he could use his pipe to play some music of his own.

Hyacinthus was amazed at the incredible beauty of Apollo, but was even more awestruck by the sound of his music, as it was like nothing a mortal had ever heard before. Hyacinthus stood and watched silently in awe. Apollo finally finished playing, and handed back the pipe, saying frankly, "I like you, Hyacinthus.' We will be friends, and you shall go with me to the palace of King Admetus."

Hyacinthus' eyes lit up; he badly wanted to go, but thinking of his duties as a shepherd, he said, " But what would become of my sheep? I must not leave them. No, no, Apollo; I cannot go with you!? " Noble youth, I love you the better because you prefer duty to pleasure; and since you cannot come with me, I will come to you. Tomorrow I will come again". True to his word, Apollo returned again; and for many long days they played, talked, and learned to love one another.

Their relationship was beautiful, and they continue to spend many days together. Unfortunately, that all ended on one fateful day when they were playing a game of discus. Hyacinthus wished that Apollo would win the game, and Apollo wished for the success of Hyacinthus.

Apollo picked up the discus, and performed a powerful throw. He would have won, but The West Wind intervened. The West Wind is a wild and gloomy fellow, and had grown jealous of their beautiful friendship. Thinking that his actions would make them quarrel, he changed the direction of the wind. The discus was blown forcefully so that it bounded back and hit Hyacinthus on the forehead, knocking him to the ground. In other versions of the story, Hyacinthus attempted to impress Apollo by trying to catch the discus, and was instead, struck in the head.

Either way, Hyacinthus took a mighty blow to the head, taking both him and Apollo by surprise. Apollo rushed toward his friend, and lifted his wounded head from the ground. Hyacinthus however was unresponsive, and his head drooped like a broken flower. Apollo wept and moaned, for Hyacinthus had died instantly from the impact. He had instantly lost his beloved friend in such a cruel and unpredictable way.

"Ah, Hyacinthus, would that I could have died for thee. My lyre shall tell of thy sad fate, and I will cause thee to be remembered, for thou art indeed a noble friend" said Apollo to his fallen companion.

Where the blood of Hyacinthus had fallen, Apollo caused to spring up the beautiful flower which bears his name, the hyacinth.

And such is the story of Hyacinthus, and of course the reason why the hyacinth flower we know today has its name.

Chapter 7: Procne & Philomena

Pandion, the King of Athens, married his maternal Aunt, Zeuxippe. Together, they had two daughters, Procne and Philomela, and also twin sons, Erechtheus and Butes. Pandion however, wasn't a great father, and was constantly preoccupied with his kingdom. When Athens went to war with Abdacus, Pandion called upon his neighbor Tereus who resided in Thrace, and asked for his help.

Tereus was not only the ruler of Daulis, he was also the son of Ares. Thanks to his many connections in Thrace, he won the war for Pandion. Pandion, being a diplomat and smart businessman, decided that Tereus should be well rewarded. He also aimed to consolidate a relationship with him, and since he was a horrible father who saw his daughters primarily as bargaining tools, gave his daughter Procne to Tereus to be his wife.

Tereus had his way with Procne, leaving her alone to take care of their son, Itys. After she was impregnated however, Tereus abandoned Procne in his house out in the country, telling nobody of her whereabouts. Then, he went to the home of Pandion, with his eyes set on Philomela. He lied to Philomela, telling her that her sister had died. He proceeded to seduce Philomela, and soon thereafter, they were married.

Upon marrying her, Tereus cut Philomena's tongue out. Philomela however, was an accomplished weaver (like many upper class Greek women were), and she wove characters into a robe in order to communicate to her sister. Once she realized that Procne was in fact alive, she sent the robe to her to let Procne know what was going on. Procne, who had until that moment been oblivious to what had happened, immediately set out to get her revenge, bringing her son, Itys, with her. Eventually, Procne found her sister, but due to her own abuse and also what she saw had been done to her sister, Procne went crazy.

Procne pretended to play along with Tereus' evilness, and told him that she would make him a magnificent dinner. She then went into the back room, where she killed her son Itys. She proceeded to boil him up, and served him to Tereus. While Tereus unknowingly feasted on his own son, Procne grabbed Philomela and ran.

Once Tereus realized that the sisters had disappeared, he took an axe and went after them. The women ran, but they were not making much ground. They prayed to the Gods to be turned into birds, and the Gods took pity upon them. Procne was transformed into the nightingale, constantly crying her sorrow in the sounds, "Itu, Itu" (the name of her son). Philomela became the voiceless swallow. Tereus was also changed into a bird, and became the hoopoe, which calls out, "pou, pou" which means "where, where" in Greek.

Chapter 8: Pygmalion & Galatea

On the island of Cyprus, lived Pygmalion, a young and extremely talented sculptor.

Pygmalion was somewhat of a woman-hater. He struggled to see the great aspects of women, and instead only took note of their multiple flaws. So it's no surprise that he resolved to never marry, and instead to focus and devote his life to his art.

Ironically enough, the masterpiece upon which he exercised the full extent of his skill was the sculpture of a woman. Perhaps, it was the result of his desire to create the perfect woman, a yardstick by which all the living women he encountered could be measured by.

For whatever reason, Pygmalion made use of all of his talent on this piece, like no other artwork he had previously created. The result was absolutely stunning, a truly beautiful work of art. Despite it's incredible design, he wasn't quite satisfied with his work. Pygmalion demanded perfection. He continued working on his female magnum opus, laboring daily, untiringly, unrelentingly, until he reached this ideal.

When at last, he was finished, the result was a wonder to behold. His piece was incomparable, for it did not even resemble a work of art. His sculptured beauty was so lifelike, at a glance she could have been mistaken for real flesh and blood.

Her beauty was unparalleled. No sculpture ever made—indeed no woman ever born—could rival her.

In the moment of her completion, womankind had their revenge upon the scornful young man, for Pygmalion had fallen in love. He had fallen in love deeply, passionately, inexplicably, with his very own creation.

It was a difficult emotion for Pygmalion to understand, for his beloved was an inanimate, lifeless thing and incapable of reciprocation—never able to kiss him, to grasp his hand, to smile, to laugh, to flush with emotion, to respond to his desire— and yet, he could not stop himself from loving her.

At first, he simply played a game of make-believe, just like a child would: he dressed her in fancy gowns, presented her with gifts, put her to bed at night and tucked her in. He would vividly imagine her reactions, and imagine how she would respond when he spoke to her; but in the end, it was never enough. He knew that he was hopelessly in love with a creation that could never possibly love him back.

Of course, the love Pygmalion expressed did not escape the attention of the goddess of love herself; none other than Aphrodite.

Pygmalion captured Aphrodite's attention, as he was a new kind of lover, afflicted by desire as so many lovers are, and yet so entirely different than the rest. He was simply original. It became Aphrodite's aim to help him out.

Cyprus, Pygmalion's home, was particularly fond of Aphrodite. It was the island that first welcomed her when she rose out of the sea foam. As such, her feast day was especially honored there. Incredible numbers of people crowded her temples, bringing gifts for her, and pleading for the goddess of love to give them success in romance.

Pygmalion attended also, but what could he possibly have asked for? He knew that it would be impossible for his masterpiece to love him back, and so he instead prayed that he might find a maiden similar to her, if that were even possible.

However, Aphrodite knew the true desire of his heart and as a sign of her favor, she made the flame of the altar in front of him leap three times. Pygmalion returned home, thoughtful of this good omen.

When he arrived home, he immediately went to find his beloved. Thinking of the omen at Aphrodite's altar, he gently caressed her and was startled in surprise—she was warm to his touch!

Doubting what he had felt, he gave her a long, lingering kiss. To his amazement and utter disbelief, he felt her cold lips grow soft and warm under his. He felt her transform as he held her: the rigidness of her limbs vanished and she softened to the touch as the stone she was carved from turned to flesh.

He held her wrists and marveled at her pulse, warm and beating under his fingertips. At last, his joy was complete, as he looked at her face and saw her smile timidly at him, her cheeks dusted pink by a maiden's innocent blush.

Pygmalion knew then what Aphrodite had done for him and his happiness and gratitude was beyond words.

Pygmalion named the maiden Galatea, and Aphrodite herself attended their wedding. Their son was named Paphos, and the goddess's favorite city was named after him.

Chapter 9: Pandora's Box

According to myth, Pandora was the first woman on earth. She was created by the order of Zeus, and was formed from clay, sculpted by Hermes. There are several different versions to this story, but what follows is the most commonly told.

Pandora was created as a punishment to humankind, in response to Prometheus stealing fire and then giving it to the humans, against Zues' orders. Pandora was given gifts from each of the Gods, from beauty, to curiosity, to musical ability. These gifts formed her personality, and created a cunning and curious woman.

Pandora was also given a box, with unknown things inside; but was instructed to never open the box. The box was filled with different evil things, that should never be released onto the world – but Pandora was created with a curious manner about her, and so she struggled to restrain herself.

Hermes took Pandora to Epimetheus, the brother of Prometheus in order to have them wed. Prometheus was not in good favor with the Gods, and had advised his brother to not accept any gifts from them. Pandora's beauty however, captivated Epimetheus, and he accepted her as his wife right away.

Pandora struggled for a while to refrain from opening the box, but eventually her curiosity prevailed. When she opened the box, all of the horrors known to humankind escaped out into the world. Strife, sickness, toil, and a range of other terrors escaped the box.

Before all of the contents escaped, Pandora was able to close the box with just one thing left inside of it – hope.

The phrase 'Pandora's box' stems from this story, and is often used to describe a taking a seemingly small and innocent action that then creates a lot of problems! When we don't know how dire the consequences will be of a small action, it is as if we opened up Pandora's box.

There are several different versions of this tale. In many, the 'box' is actually referred to as a jar. The changing of the story to a 'box' only occurred in the 16th century, when it was translated to Latin. Since then, the phrase 'Pandora's box' has grown famous.

In some versions of the story, the jar or box was actually in the possession of Epimetheus already, and Pandora found it in his home.

Regardless of the exact version of events, the key components of the story remain the same. Zeus wanted to punish the humans, and did so by creating the first woman and making her overly curious, cunning, and not so trustworthy.

Chapter 10: The Epics

There are Greek myths, and then there are the epics.

An epic is a mythological story that is told in the form of a series of poems or stanzas, and it's believed that they were originally oral histories that were later transcribed and might even have been by multiple authors, although the two most famous epics are generally attributed to the work of a poet named Homer.

The two epics that are the most enduring and well-known are the Iliad, and the Odyssey. The first tells the story of the Trojan War, and the second tells the story of what happens to the surviving Greeks after the war.

These two accounts are generally fictional, but contain actual historical events. For example, there really was a war between Troy and Greece, and in fact, there might have been multiple ones. However, the reasons for the war and the people involved were probably exaggerated, as was the involvement of the gods to explain the tide turning in the favor of one side over another.

The Iliad tells of how the Trojan War begins when Hecate, envious of the other gods, throws a golden apple into the feast for the gods that reads "for the fairest." Athena, Hera, and Aphrodite all claim the apple, and it is decided that Paris, a Prince of Troy, will decide which of them it is. Each goddess offers Paris a prize in return for him choosing them.

Paris chooses Aphrodite, who promises him the love of the most beautiful woman in the world, Helen. Helen is already married, but Paris steals her away and brings her back to Troy. As a result, Agamemnon, the brother of Helen's husband Menelaus, declares war on Troy.

The Greeks proceed to surround Troy and lay siege, starving Troy's citizens. There are various heroic deeds during this time, most importantly Achilles on the Greek side and Hector on the Trojan side. The war finally ends when Odysseus, with help from Athena, devises the idea of the Trojan Horse.

The Greeks claim that they are going home and erect a massive horse as an offering to Poseidon to ask for his help on the journey across the sea. They ask that the Trojans leave the horse alone. The Trojans, however, bring the horse into the city to burn it to bring bad luck to the Greeks—as Athena told Odysseus they would. Hidden inside the horse is the Greek army, and they burst out, destroying the city and taking Helen back home.

The Odyssey tells the story of how Odysseus sets off home with the rest of the Greek army, but ends up murdering a cyclops, one of Poseidon's children. This angers Poseidon and as god of the sea, he is able to delay Odysseus coming home by ten years, encountering many dangers and monsters along the way, including Scylla, the many-headed monster, and Charybdis, a swirling whirlpool.

These epics are still often quoted and referenced today and served as inspiration for many classical authors afterwards. They are multilayered stories that have multiple chapters and cover many characters and span over a period of years. Most myths are simpler stories, or various smaller stories that can later be pieced together, such as the stories about the exploits of Hercules.

The epics truly introduced to civilization the mythological tales that would later become novels, setting them above most other myths and putting them on the list of classic literature.

Chapter 11: The Legacy Of The Greeks

Greek myths are some of the most enduring in the world. They continue into the present day, with animated films such as Disney's Hercules, and in television shows such as American Gods and Atlantis.

When you mention mythology to someone, a good chance is that the first stories and characters that they'll mention will be those of Ancient Greece.

The Greeks were partially enduring because of the huge strides that they made in science and technology. Their history and culture were a huge influence in the western world, and so it makes sense that as their history and technology were so pervasive, their myths would be as well.

It's also because their stories are so honestly entertaining. Gods that backstab and sleep with one another and can turn into animals, men who go to war, and women with magic who trick, or seduce, or gain power as they will? It's very much like modern-day soap operas, only with more magic involved.

If you look around, you'll be surprised at how much the Greek myths continue to be a part of our everyday lives. They're in our sayings, such as when you tell your friend that a task is herculean, or when you say that a cake is tantalizing. They're in our media, including companies: the popular sports equipment company Nike gets its name from the goddess of victory. The Iliad and the Odyssey, Homer's two epics, are considered classical literature and are read as novels, still studied today for their symbolism and character arcs. Percy Jackson and the Olympians, one of the most popular young adult book series in recent years, is about the Greek gods in modern times.

It's almost paramount that one becomes familiar with Greek mythology if only so that one can understand the references that we make to them in film, television, literature, and our everyday lives. The ancient Greeks might be long gone, but their influence and stories are here to stay. And what interesting, entertaining, stories they are.

Conclusion

Thanks again for taking the time to read this book!

You should now have a good understanding of Greek Mythology. I hope you enjoyed learning about the many characters and stories that were a part of the Ancient Greek culture.

If you enjoyed this book, please take the time to leave me a review on Amazon. I appreciate your honest feedback, and it really helps me to continue producing high quality books.